Table Of Contents

Acknowledgements

I want to extend my thanks to a few people who helped me bring this book to completion. It took a lot of work and I could not have done it without the support of my business partners and business coach along with the great people in our mastermind.

Thank you to my amazing wife, Adriane, who helped a lot with the social media portion of this book. She is very knowledgable about that topic and is a great asset to have and I am grateful for her contribution.

Thank you to my father, Terry, helped with editing and I am grateful for his contribution and encouragement as I went through the process.

Thank you to Jon Toy, my business coach, who has given me some great guidance throughout this process. As an author himself he was able to help me stay on track and provide very useful advice.

And thanks to my mom, Anita, for being a loving, caring and thoughtful mom!

Introduction

I want to start by giving you some background and why you should, as a business owner or manager, read this book. You might not know who I am, or if you do, you may not know much about me. You're probably wondering why you should believe anything in this book. I respect that. It was 1999 when I first started helping companies succeed online with website development, search engine optimization (SEO) then, finally, social media marketing and management. My team and I have helped hundreds of businesses with all aspects of their online presence through the years. Now, we only refer to those aspects as an online reputation.

Throughout this book, I give examples on how to manage your online reputation the correct way, and also, how to do it incorrectly. At the end of the book, there is a free reputation snapshot report for your business as a thank you for taking the time to read this. My mission and the purpose of this book is to help as many businesses improve their overall online reputation as possible.

Background

When I started JAZ Design Company it was 1999. A lot was different back then with how the internet worked. The Internet was a place to post information about your business, and it was in the form of what we now refer to as Web 1.0. There was a one-way direction for all content being posted. The search engines were just coming about,as well as the indexing of content that was being posted. I first learned about Google at the end of 1999. Other search engines were more popular back then, but Google just seemed to work the best.

Since then, the internet has continued to evolve, and the way we use it has too. I remember back in the early 2000's when the phrase "Search Engine Optimization" was first coined. People were spamming the search engines any way they knew how. It was like the Wild West out there, and in hindsight, I wish I would have done a lot of things differently such as leveraging the power of the internet for placing ads and selling products. It isn't as easy anymore to just post a Google AdWords ad and get instant traffic to your page where you sell survival kits and make millions.

It's worth mentioning how the web evolved since 1999 when I first started working in this industry. The internet started with what is referred to as Web 1.0. Back then, web pages were a place for people to go and read information that was posted by the publishers of the content. These publishers were the only people who could contribute to the pages, and they were static unless changed by the owner with access to them.

Most pages were personal web pages hosted on local ISP servers or sites like Geocities. This was the era of Myspace, later Facebook. Personal blogs were very popular, and people used sites like BlogSpot to create accounts to publish content. These were platforms for readers to comment on the pages. This started the new generation of Web 2.0.

The Web 2.0 capabilities are present, but they were slightly different from what we know them to be today. Instead of the comments area we are familiar with today, it was more of a guestbook posting area. We moved from personal sites to a new type of website that holds a lot more participation capabilities for readers. This completely changed how we use the internet. We now have the ability to tag others and create a much wider reach with our engagement online, which is the fundamental change realized with the concept of Web 2.0, and another main reason why I'm writing this book.

Businesses now have the ability to use this reach to market and build brand recognition because of the two-way conversations we are able to have with our customers and prospects. Now, it is the job of a business to educate and entertain through any and all platforms they are using. The many different platforms based on the company niche make this possible. We can identify where our ideal customers are hanging out, and then join the conversation in a way that is engaging and exciting. If you can gain trust by getting your ideal customers to know, like and trust you online through social media, videos, and blogs, the sales process becomes much more effective than using old outbound media like billboards and TV commercials.

Let's dig in and look at how we can use the internet effectively for our businesses, while leveraging the tools that exist to do this well.

Part 1:

What Is Reputation Management?

Chapter 1:
Defining Reputation Management

"It takes 20 years to build a reputation and five minutes to ruin it. If you think about that, you'll do things differently." – Warren Buffet

What is reputation management? It's vital because it's the center of your entire internet presence. In simpler terms, it's a part of your advertising and should be part of your overall budget.

Your reputation is surrounded by your website, which is essentially your face on the internet. Your online presence is influenced by social media, how you engage with your audience online, and your potential clients. It's also about your search presence for those looking at what your company has to offer.

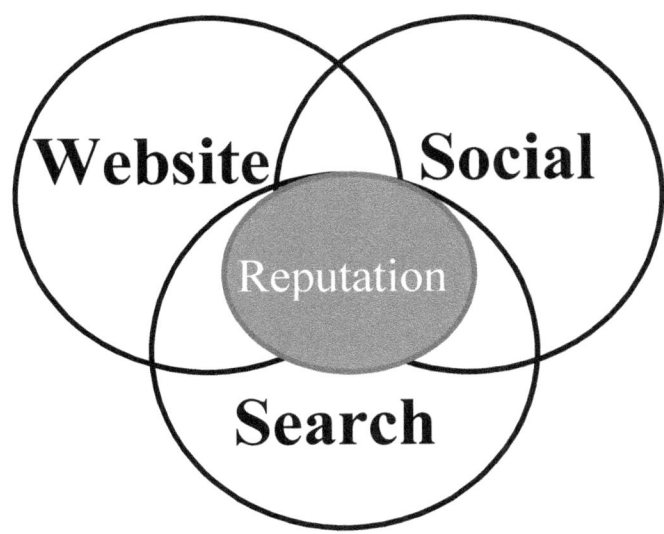

- Can you be found on search engines?

- Is the data that exists online about your business correct?

- Are you active on social media?

- Do you know if you have reviews on major review websites?

In order to develop important connections, you can post comments on forums to interact with people. Eventually, they will begin to like you because you've given them some advice and have gained their trust. Whether it's negative or positive, reviews are costing businesses thousands of dollars. One bad review can lead to thousands of dollars in lost revenue.

If you are doing any type of advertising for your business, whether it's on TV, radio, SEO, or pay-per-click advertising (PPC), you better have a good reputation. What's going to happen is once people see your advertisement, they may or may not decide to do business with you right away like we did years ago.

REPUTATION MANAGEMENT
Stop losing new customers to bad reviews

The buyer behavior has changed significantly, and the prospective customer will more likely Google you than anything else. Think about it, if you have a bunch of bad reviews out there - that you may or may not know exist, potential customers will move onto the next company that is similar to yours, but with a better reputation. It happens every day.

Most of the people that I talk to, who own small businesses, have reviews on Google Business (Google+) or Yelp that they've never even seen, and they're usually bad. No kidding.

If you read a bad review and you've never done business with somebody before, you will likely never do business with them at all. Because of that ONE person who left a bad review that you didn't even know existed, your business could lose thousands of dollars in revenue. Even if they do not spend thousands themselves, you will lose money on potential word of mouth sales from their friends and family members. If one customer's lifetime value is $500 to $1,000, you can imagine how much this will cost the company if 10-100 people read that bad review.

The virtual doorway of your business on the internet is essentially two things. What you say about yourself online, and what data exists about you out there. Every business holds a digital footprint online. This 'trail' contains all the data about your business that exists on different websites called directory websites. These particular sites list data for most businesses in the world. Your footprint is also what Google has out there about your business. Google did every business a favor by giving them a free page about their business.

For most, however, it isn't doing them any favors. The problem is that they created this webpage for their business that the business owner has no idea exists. This Google+ page is a place to list information about businesses, as well as a place to for customers to leave reviews. Since most business owners have not claimed these listings or updated them, they are, in many cases, unaware that there are reviews from past customers. Unfortunately, most of the time, the reviews are negative.

> *You wouldn't give your business card out with the wrong phone number on it would you?*

Not monitoring and fixing business listing data is like handing out a business card with the wrong information on it. We wouldn't go to a networking event and give out a business card that has the wrong phone number or email address on it. However, that's what is happening for many businesses online. They have inconsistent and inaccurate listing data that is causing them to lose business. Since the search engines include how accurate business listing data is in their algorithm, this problem is also affecting businesses' search engine positioning.

The other aspect of the digital footprint is what others are saying about you. Customers are controlling the conversation. The only way a business owner can take the reins back is through reputation management. This consists of updating business listing data and monitoring feedback.

The vast amount of information about products and services online has changed the way people buy. So if, for example, I see an ad for a local dentist, I know that's paid propaganda by the dentist. The dentist paid to put it out there because they want me to go to them when I need a dentist. If I read reviews from people that have been to that dentist, and they all say they love it, I'm probably going to trust their comments a lot more than the ad.

Buyer Behavior – Bad Reviews

Buyer Behavior is changing. It's not at all what it used to be. Everyone is following the old adage "The customer is always right." Even though this causes customers to take advantage of companies, we can still create a balanced conversation. The trick is to learn to take that control back without the commenters even realizing it.

Rita McCann
The Extra Big Smiles dental Clinic is the worst. I waited forever, the hygenist was rude and the dentist did not know what she was doing! I will never go back!

Like • Comment • Share   2 hours ago

👍 3 people like this.

Sheila Wright You must have gone on a bad day, because I have had nothing but positive experiences! I have been going here for almost 7 years and love it every time - try again!
1 hour ago • Like

Val Sander No way! My whole family goes here and they are the absolute BEST! I used to dread going to the dentist and now I love it
38 minutes ago • Like

Essentially, the virtual doorway of your company is your reputation. This is just one example of the several types of conversations that are going on right now on the web. This person named Rita had a bad experience at a local dentist, so she wanted to let her friends know about it on her favorite social media platform.

In this example, we see that two of her friends are the dentist's brand ambassadors. They shared their opinion in order to give the business another chance. Essentially, your customers are your brand ambassadors, so treat them right.

In the next example, even though the review is old, people can find it and read it. We encouraged the Jewelry store to comment on it. People use these reviews every day to decide if they want to do business with someone or not. We use the reviews to decide if a product or service is good. This is how potential customers make up their mind about buying decisions.

If you have a lot of good reviews, but your business listing information is not accurate (people cannot find your phone number to call you, or they drive to the wrong address), then the sale is most likely gone forever. The potential customer moves on to the next business that has kept up with their online reputation. Boom – your competitor now has a sale that could have been yours! Social platforms are the new word of word-of-mouth, since they allow people to leave comments and have conversations like we used to do at the local watering holes.

Rita McCann
ABC We Buy Houses practically stole my house from me and I am disappointed in the experience because I could have made more money if I would have fixed it up and listed it my self.

Like • Comment • Share   2 hours ago

👍 3 people like this.

Sheila Wright I ran the numbers myself and I found that I wouldn't have made much more and it would have taken me months to fix my mothers house and I just didn't have the time or knowledge. I am happy they helped me with the house.

1 hour ago • Like

Val Sander No way! They were great to work with and saved me a lot of hassle and I wouldn't have made any more money considering the work it needed.

38 minutes ago • Like

In another example, a person named Sue said the following on her favorite social media platform about ABC We Buy Houses: "They practically stole my house from me. I'm disappointed in the experience because I could have made more money if I would have fixed it up and listed it myself."

Now, we can easily see how the word "stole" can give ABC We Buy Houses a negative reputation. Most people would have enough common sense to see that she was the one who made the decision to sell her home. No one forced her to sell it. She was the one who could have stated that she wanted more money at the beginning, before the transaction was made and the deal was done. But, in hindsight, she felt she should have negotiated a higher price. She didn't, and, in the end, she blamed the real estate company.

Now, we all know that this is very wrong. But people do it ALL THE TIME. Most people would look at the comment and realize that she was just upset, and was taking her anger out on the company, posting comments online for EVERYONE to see. But not everyone has common sense. Many people are apt to take another person's word like it's rock solid! This is unfortunate, but something a business can't run from. We cannot control what others take away from online reviews.

The company might be able to get her on the phone and say, "I ran the numbers myself and I found that you would not have made more money because you would've had to put your own money in it to fix it up, and you have no idea how much you would have been able to sell it for. Just because you put thousands of dollars into your home to fix it up, does not mean that you can increase the selling price by that much. It would have taken you months to fix the house. The time you spent would have taken away from other work you could've been doing at the time to make money." Time = Money.

This is a fictitious example, but illustrates an important point about how consumers are swaying the conversation, thus becoming brand ambassadors. In utilizing these conversations we are now considered content marketers by implementing a few promotional factors. We can start to steer the conversations that are happening and, at the same time, provide value.

When you provide value by answering questions, solving problems, or asking more questions to trigger additional thoughts in a consumer's mind, which may propel them to make a purchase, then your reputation management attempts are not futile. This is where social media marketing will help you reach, or maybe even surpass your overall marketing goals. Giving content and value to the followers of your business can go a long way toward brand recognition and building a positive vibe around your business. Make it fun and unique in some way. People will then pay attention and share your content. This will, in turn, build your brand.

What we need to do is monitor and manage reviews like this. There are three steps to dealing with reviews. The first step is to say you're sorry. If it's a bad review, just say you're sorry, even if you're not sorry, because, as we stated earlier - the customer's always right. The second thing to do is to say,

"This must be an isolated incident. We don't have a lot of other bad reviews." The third thing you say is, "I'm the owner" or "I'm the manager. Here's my phone number and email address. Please call or email me so we can work this out".

This does two things. Number one, it shows potential customers that you do care and tried to get the person on the phone. This is key, because the only person that can take down a bad review is the person that left it. So work with them, and try to get the comment taken down.

Number two, by responding, it shows that you care and want to make the customer happy. As a result of failing to ignore these bad reviews, you develop a good customer service reputation.

Number three, you are acknowledging the problem. You are showing the customer that their feelings matter. You are also letting them know that it's an isolated incident.

Those three pieces of advice are vital, so take notes and remember them!

Getting Malicious Reviews/Mentions Removed From Google

Have you ever Googled yourself or your business? It is interesting to find what comes up. If you are in a high level position, you should be aware of any possible negativity. There are likely mentions of your business you didn't know about.

What if some of these mentions are malicious? This is a big problem for some people and companies who have competition or have had an unhappy customer. When you search your name, or your business name, the majority of the results should be content that belongs to you. If this is not the case, follow the advice in this book for creating content around your brand.

If there is a bad review on Google, an incorrect mention of you, or your business, there are 2 things that can be done. You can flag the inappropriate review which will alert Google to review it. The other thing you can do if they don't take it down is to get a court order in your favor. This order can be submitted to Google through a process they have laid out on their website.

Google has a "Legal Removal Request" area that guides you through the process to remove content for good. This is where you can submit the court order for defamation of character. To be sure the process goes smoothly, you might want to consult an attorney who specializes in this.

Buyer Behavior – Good Reviews

What about good reviews? We want to ask for feedback so we can get more good reviews, because it is rare to come across a customer that spends the extra time to tell the world about their good buying experience. In order to receive more positive feedback, always ask your customers to leave reviews. As business owners, we need to engage with them in order to take that next step. We need to help them ultimately understand, like and trust our business brand. Incorporate it into your sales process. When the customer has finished the transaction and is happy, ask them to leave feedback. Get their email address and send them a link to the review site you are trying to populate with good reviews. This is something they can do in a minute or two. Also, you will likely get a fifteen to twenty percent conversion rate, which is better than you are likely doing now.

On the other hand, what about reviews that exist currently? Businesses are ignoring the bad reviews that have been sitting on the web for eternity. It's an epidemic when you think about it. We would never ignore people coming into our store who have a complaint, so why are we doing it online? When people leave good reviews, we need to harvest this user generated content, and encourage customers to leave reviews on a Google+ page, Facebook page, or Yelp. Afterward, simply publish those reviews. If it's a good review, use it. If they left it on Google +, copy it, and put it on your Facebook. With good reputation management software, you can easily follow up with customers with an email. When it is submitted, the review will be available online automatically. This should be incorporated into every sales process to increase the number of good reviews.

You can get good reviews another way, however. You can create a slew of fictitious accounts to start leaving reviews for your company yourself. Or, you can hire a company to do that for you. I would really advise against it, because a company was fined $350,000 by the Attorney General for doing just that. So, please stay away from this strategy.

Give Yourself 5 Stars? Online, It Might Cost You

By DAVID STREITFELD
Published: September 22, 2013   316 Comments

"I celebrate myself, and sing myself," wrote Walt Whitman, America's great bard of self-promotion. As the world goes ever more digital, quite a few businesses are adopting that philosophy — hiring a veritable chorus of touts to sing their nonexistent praises and lure in customers.

Nathaniel Brooks for The New York Times
Eric T. Schneiderman, the New York attorney general, called the deceptions "worse than old-fashioned false advertising."

Reviewing the Review Reviewers

Monday's article about a crackdown on fake reviewing prompted many responses from readers indicating that the problem is even worse than regulators think.

· Give Yourself 5 Stars? Online, It Might Cost You

New York regulators will announce on Monday the most comprehensive crackdown to date on deceptive reviews on the Internet. Agreements have been reached with 19 companies to cease their misleading practices and pay a total of $350,000 in penalties.

The yearlong investigation encompassed companies that create fake reviews as well as the clients that buy them. Among those signing the agreements are a charter bus operator, a teeth-whitening service, a laser hair-removal chain and an adult entertainment club. Also signing are several reputation-enhancement firms that place fraudulent reviews on sites like Google, Yelp, Citysearch and Yahoo.

A phony review of a restaurant may lead to a bad meal, which is disappointing. But the investigation uncovered a wide range of services buying fake reviews that could do more permanent damage: dentists, lawyers, even an ultrasound clinic.

Where are people leaving reviews these days? Google+, Facebook, Yelp, AngiesList and more. Facebook is accepting reviews as well, and they have three times more business reviews than Yelp. Google Business Pages (Google+) are extremely popular, because they come up when looking for local businesses. When you do a search for a local business, it's the Google Business (Google+) page that pops up first. Google Business (Google+) is great, and it's an easy place to leave reviews for a company. The problem is, most business owners don't know about their page, have not claimed it, or have unknown reviews. Remember, it is human nature to want to complain about a bad experience, but move on when a good experience is expected.

Online reviews equal money. 90% of buying decisions are influenced by online reviews. That's a lot of people. I've seen statistics down to 60%, but, essentially, there's a lot of people that look at reviews. Reviews are a trusted part of the buying process. Remember that trust is the bedrock to a company's brand identity.

For example, if I see a product or service that has a lot of five star reviews, I'm probably going to say, "Well, a bunch of people reviewed it. They gave it five stars, so I'm just going to buy it. I have no reason to waste more time and do any more digging. I trust these reviews."

Reputation Monitoring

The internet is a social platform thanks to Web 2.0 as explained above, but how do we use that for promoting our business and getting ahead of our competitors in the search engines? That is the fundamental question: what return will I get on my investment of time and money to manage and monitor my overall reputation online? The answer to that is of course, it depends.

For most business owners, dealing with the negative reviews will save them a lot in lost revenue. The data that is erroneous and inconsistent causes business listings to be pushed down in the search results. This is because legitimacy and consistent, accurate data is priority number one for search engines.

Real Life Example

Let's first look at a real life example of a bad review that, in my estimation, cost a local audiologist thousands of dollars in lost revenue. We don't know the exact amount that was lost, but we do know that it was a substantial amount, and an example that we can all learn from.

Someone who had a bad experience at this practice went ahead and wrote a bad review on Yelp. The business was not at fault. In fact, they tried everything they could to make the cost affordable to the patient. However, there was no way the cost could be deferred, so the service was refused. It happens all the time. In this case, the patient did what most humans naturally do. She complained where everyone could see, on a major review site.

My client called me one day in a panic and showed me the review. At that point it had been 7 months since it was posted. Of course, we were not monitoring and managing her reputation at the time, so we had no idea it was out there either. The long review, probably over 300 words, was horrible and anyone who read it would think the practice was horrible as well.

This patient was very articulate in their wording and made a lot of damaging attacks toward the practice. The worst part is that the button below the review that says, "Did you find this review helpful," was clicked 9 times. An estimate of the number of people who read that review is about ten times the number of people who took the initiative to click the button, so perhaps 90 people were swayed by that review and will never do business there.

If you read a bad review of a business that you have never been to before, will you ever go there? Probably not. Since then, we have been monitoring her reputation every day, and whenever something pops up, for example, like on her Facebook page, we know about it and can respond to it properly.

Right away, the three step response was made to mitigate the negative effects of the review, and, ultimately, get the person who wrote it to take it down. When you have 3 reviews on Facebook, one of which is from the business (not such a great idea), and the other two are from customers - one is 3 stars, the other is 5 stars, this can have an effect on attracting new customers in a negative way. Social media is part of your regular existence online, so make sure you have a presence or a proof of your existence. Are there social accounts for your business? Are they being used or setup properly?

If they are setup by you or someone else, they should be optimized for both users and search engines. Your social profiles help rank your business in search results, so information should be correct.

Do you have bad reviews and inconsistent listing data? Visit www.yourlastreview.com to get a free reputation snapshot and find out.

Chapter 2:
The New Buyer Behavior

"Unfortunately, your reputation often rests not on your ability to do what you say, but rather on your ability to do what people expect." – Bryant H. McGill

Buyer behavior has completely changed, so reputation management is more important than ever. Instead of purchasing a product or a service first and asking questions later, now everyone is asking questions first and purchasing later. The number of small and medium sized business in the U.S. has increased dramatically over the recent years. There are both good and bad companies out there.

In the past, when we were ready to buy, we used to go to the store and talk to the salesperson who would explain the various products they offered and sell you on the benefits. Now, it's the opposite experience, since everyone has the internet to do their research before entering the store. If there are 5 stores selling the same thing in the mall, which one are you going to go in? The one that looks the best, correct?

Customer expectations are high, and unless we exceed those expectations each time, it will be difficult to gain their trust. Trust is the foundation of a business brand.

For example, after placing an order, the business offering the product will tell you that your package will arrive within one week, when they know that you're going to receive it 2 days early and be pleasantly shocked. Even if the faster shipping charge is hidden in the price of the item, the customer will never know! This is not bad business or deceitful. In this day and age, we have to take desperate measures to make sure customers' unspoken demands are met. The same goes for reputation management.

Customer Service is one way a person's reputation becomes golden or rotten. You don't necessarily have to hire a customer service representative in order to provide the best Customer Service - unless your company is large enough that you can no longer handle the job on your own. As far as basic customer service goes, that can easily be incorporated into your reputation management package – if you have one, or will be subscribing to one in the future. When a customer leaves a review, we want to make sure we try to work it out. Put yourself in your customers' shoes.

Chapter 3:
Being Transparent

Because of how easy it is for people to research and have access to new information, transparency is something we should embrace as business owners. Since anyone can post anything they want online about anything, it is important to be monitoring the activity and conversations that surround our businesses. If someone posts a review on the major review websites or on a blog comment, we want to see what that says.

If it is good, we can use it as a post on Facebook. If it is bad, we want to be on top of it and make sure we're dealing with it as soon as possible to mitigate the harmful effects of a bad review. Reviews and comments are ways we can engage with our audience. This is something many business owners are ignoring or are simply unaware of. Let's start paying attention and talking to customers, so we can harvest this data and use it to our advantage.

We have direct access to the audience who are active on these platforms from, practically, any device, yet we are not taking advantage of the ease that technology has brought into our lives. Through ads we can target specific types of people with specific interests, but we will talk more about that later.

You want to be completely transparent. You might be trying to hide from the rest of the world, and you think that no one notices, but that's not true at all. People are going to talk no matter what. You will find all sorts of conversations online. You definitely want to be a part of the conversation, but in a good way.

Reputation Management isn't about getting rid of the negative comments.This is impossible unless you contact the person who left them and convinced them to take it down. If you're able to please the unhappy customer, ask for them to reconsider keeping up the negative comments. What they're saying about you will be there for a long time – probably forever. An immediate response is vital, but you must continue to monitor it as well. Others will begin to chime in, but you must cut them off at the pass, so that bell never rings.

Platforms

Where do we find these comments and reviews? We want to look at the platforms where our ideal clients and audience are hanging out. There are many different types of platforms, so decide which ones you want to use and stick to those. Add more as you become better at managing them, but don't try to do everything at once, unless you are able to hire a social media manager. Thankfully, there are companies who can manage both your reputation and your social media accounts. They both go hand in hand.

So, what is reputation and how is it affected by social media? It's a part of your overall existence. Here are some questions you need to ask yourself before getting started. Is there proof of your existence out there? What do I mean by that? Firstly, do you have Facebook, Twitter, and other social media accounts? Do you have activity on those accounts? Are your social media accounts being used? Are you posting to those?

Reviews, comments, and engagement are all things that we have to be concerned with when thinking about our overall reputation online, because people are always commenting. They are also reviewing our businesses and services when they do business with us. We have faster access to more people than ever before in the history of mankind. We are able to access people according to their interests. Facebook delves into this new analytical tool nicely.

However, I'm going to explain Facebook ads and how they're really important later.

We can immediately correspond with whoever we want to. We can private message people on Facebook. We can tweet them. We can, essentially, text them. Everybody has a mobile device that they're able to use to do that. Social media can be delivered to many different platforms. We need to determine which platforms make the most sense, because we don't necessarily want to be active on all of them. That is, unless we hire a social media manager, because it's just going to take up too much of our time.

There are also industry specific social media platforms like REI Blackbook. That is a specific social network for real estate investors. Forums are also a place that you can go to establish the like and trust factor with your customers.

Part 2:

Why The Internet Is A Social Platform And How To Make It Work For Your Business

Chapter 4:
Reviews

Reviews are probably the most influential place where businesses are affected and should give their full attention to. This is because reviews are the new word of mouth. As consumers of products from amazon.com to finding the local plumber on angieslist.com, we have come to rely on these reviews to make our buying decisions.

People have changed the way they buy products and services. Personally, I use reviews every time I buy something on Amazon to figure out which similar product for a similar price performs best.

Historically, we asked our friends, or took advice from the manufacturers' commercials we watched on TV to make our buying decisions. Now, there is an immense amount of data that can be used for determining where our money is best spent. Another way reviews can be used by businesses is to get feedback for product improvement and marketing. If there are a lot of complaints about a specific product your competitor makes, why not use that data to improve your product?

Market research is not very fun, but it's absolutely necessary if you have goals to become a profitable, successful company. Customer reviews from other similar companies are a large part of market research. The initial split testing phase takes time and money, but it is absolutely worth the investment. Use the data that's already available in order to make the product meet most people's expectations during the beginning phase of a product launch.

Are you blocking or ignoring the virtual front or of your business on the internet? You can request a free reputation snapshot of your business at www.yourlastreview.com. You may not know how you're blocking the entrance to your business. We can see from the outside in, using a detailed report with a high level summary to see at a glance. It's enlightening and interesting as you will learn how to easily monitor reviews, and how to build your online reputation (legally).

Inconsistent online business data can lead to thousands in lost revenue. It's not just a review; it's really all of your internet assets. Your reputation is in the middle of your website, your social presence, and your search engine optimization. It really brings everything together. The website is where people find you. It needs to be mobile friendly, because over 60% of all internet traffic is done on a mobile device these days.

Social media is where you engage with your ideal customers and clients. Where are they hanging out online? The web has become more of a social engagement platform, rather than going there to find information like in the past. Now, people are engaging a lot more. The search engines have a lot of data about your company. Is all of it accurate and are you able to be found there? Those are the big things we want to look at.

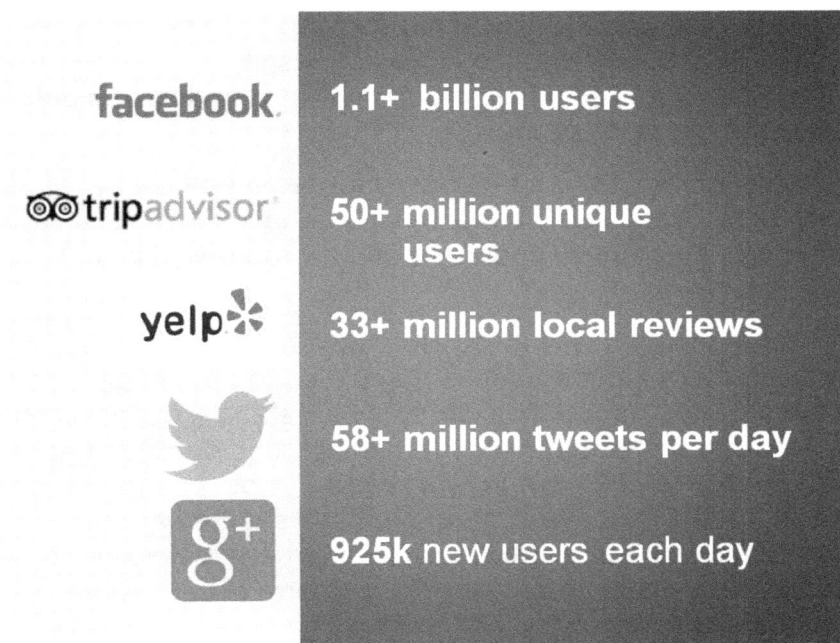

facebook. 1.1+ billion users

tripadvisor 50+ million unique users

yelp 33+ million local reviews

58+ million tweets per day

g+ 925k new users each day

Purchasing Decisions

With the advent of mobile devices, everyone has a computer in their pocket that they use to research everything they want before making a purchasing decision. Before they leave their house, and while they are in their car, they're going to their mobile device before doing business with a company they don't know all too well or at all.

Mobile phones have changed online buying behavior. Before, we used to go in the store and talk to the salesperson to decide what we wanted. Now, we are researching it, then going to the place to do business. Life as we knew it has completely changed.

If you walk into the store and find something you want to buy, you can do two things with your mobile device. You can attempt to find coupons before purchasing, or you can look at the price on Amazon. If it's cheaper online, you will wait to make the purchase until you get back home. You can also look at reviews while at the store, but, especially, beforehand. 83% of shoppers said they made their buying decision before actually entering a store.

Companies wonder why their businesses aren't the same as they were years ago. Typical buying behavior is not so typical anymore. This is why your reputation is more vital now than it was years ago.

What I mean by this is, because customer service is outsourced to other countries, people become enraged when they talk to someone they cannot understand – especially here in America. Instead of making a split second decision backed with confidence in a brand or a product, most people are now waiting until they have assurance that what they are purchasing will be trustworthy. This is where reviews come in, and why reputation management is a form of customer service.

How to Turn Online Reviews Into Cash

Online reviews equal cash. In a recent survey by Nielsen, 90% of buyers said their buying decision was influenced by online reviews. These are really interesting statistics. The amount of new businesses with positive reviews that can't convert when compared with companies with zero or negative reviews is 183%. That's staggering. When someone sees a place that is ranked 4.5 out of 5 stars, they're probably thinking that's a really good business, and they'll most likely do business with them without even thinking about it. We've come to rely on these reviews, because the world of business reputation has become a social network.

70%	Customers who read consumer reviews to ensure they are purchasing the right product or service.
90%	US customers who say their buying decisions are influenced by online reviews.
183%	The amount of new business companies with positive reviews can convert when compared to companies with ZERO or negative reviews.
82%	Consumers who consider user generated reviews important or extremely important.

How To (How We) Deal With Business Reviews

How do we deal with business reviews? Every business falls into one of these three categories: They have no reviews, they have negative reviews, or they have a lot of good reviews, but they aren't managing them properly. We have a solution for all three of these categories, and I'm going to explain what to do for each one.

The first thing you need to do is be aware of reviews that are out there about your business. It is important that we do not this negative or positive word of mouth just sit there without engaging. Many business owners used to think no one was checking the internet for reviews. In the last few years, everybody is going online.

What would you do if somebody came into your store and had a complaint? You wouldn't just say, "Oh, I don't really want to talk to you, so I'm going to go over here to my office." You would talk to them and try to work it out. Businesses that are ignoring their reviews online are, essentially, ignoring their customers. Why would anyone do this? It's not on purpose. Time is very limited, and there is no one available to manage the reviews.

Here is one example: One customer gave a business two stars because, even though they got an adequate haircut, they also had some other problems. The business owner did the right thing. She said, "I'm sorry you had a bad experience. We've been cutting hair for over 15 years." Essentially, she was trying to work it out with the customer. Somebody who reads this review sees that the business owner cares. That's going to reduce the negative effects of the review. The only person that can take a negative review down is the person that put it up, so we always try to work it out with the original commenter.

Through another example, we will show you exactly how to respond to a negative review. The first thing you want to do if someone is not happy is to say you're sorry. Say something like, "I'm really sorry you had a negative experience. We really pride ourselves in doing a good job with customer service. Then, mention that this must be an isolated incident, because, normally, people rave about our customer service." Let them know their bad experience is uncommon and that you want to take steps to fix it. Then, tell them to call you. Say, "My name is Jason. I'm the owner. You can reach me at this number."

Now, we've shown everybody that we're really trying to work it out with this person. That's the benefit of review management. Like I said, the only person who can take the review down is the person who put it up, so it's vital to be engaging. To recap, say you're sorry, mention something about it being an isolated incident, "this is uncommon," then get the customer on the phone. You can even tell them to leave their number if you cannot find it in your records. Call them to show that you're being pro-active about the problem. Finally, the only person who can take down a review is the person who left it.

Harvest User Generated Content

The other thing we need to do is harvest user generated content. Word of mouth is a more common way to think about it. User generated content is word of mouth online. Encourage your customers, patients, and clients to leave online reviews, and then use those reviews on your social media and website. If somebody leaves a good review, post that on your Facebook page or tweet about it. This is going to show a lot of people that your business is successful in maintaining a good experience with your customers. When they're ready to buy, they will feel comfortable coming back to do business with you again.

Positive reviews are tough to get, so we need to both ask for them and then respond to them, and thanking them when we see them. They're rare, because when people buy something and have a good experience, they move on quickly. They don't take further action, necessarily, because they are enjoying their purchase. They don't feel like they should do anything, because they expected to have that good experience they expected to have.

On the other hand, a negative experience will cause a customer to go out of their way and spend extra time to tell everyone they know that they had that experience. We need to take care of the positive ones and reinforce that good behavior as well. When someone leaves a review, say something like, "We love when customers have an awesome experience. Thanks for your review. Here is something else you might enjoy," and send them some information or a gift.

The Magic 3 in Google Local Results

There are three things every business needs. First, it's extremely vital that you create a Google Business page. Even if Google Business (Google+) pages are not all that popular from a social media standpoint yet, Google still rules the internet. If you play by their rules, you will get a lot farther in terms of your business goals. Google reviews really help, because it makes your listing stand out. Consistent listing data on Google is not something you want your business to be without. We will talk more about business listing data in the next chapter (Ch.6).

Indulge Salon
3.9 ★★★★ (14) · Beauty Salon
970 S George St · (717) 846-4424
Closed today

Website   Directions

Iridescence Salon & Spa
3 reviews · Day Spa
1412 E Market St · (717) 751-4444
Closed today

Website   Directions

Creations Hair Salon
2 reviews · Beauty Salon
351 Loucks Rd · (717) 846-6040

Directions

☰ More hair salon

When we did a search for salons, it delivered 3 with the most consistent listing data, along with a Google+ page. When you have a review, it helps to really boost it, because Google looks at all of the listing data that it can possibly find. Because Google wants to provide the best user experience, if it sees inconsistencies with that, it's going to place your competitor that has more consistent data above your listing.

When a customer receives the top 3 results on Google, their experience is comparable to a shopping mall, where everyone is attempting to deliver the best experience – competing for your attention and ultimately your business. A potential customer, obviously, will look through the listings and choose the one that looks the absolute best. If their first choice doesn't match up, they'll keep looking down the list until they find something that is comparable. This is exactly what online users are doing. You do not want to get skipped – even if you are 1st on the list! The 1st, 2nd, and 3rd listings could easily be tied for 1st place, but you would never know that because the order implicates that one is better than the other. This is not always true.

Imagine if there were five customers outside of your store and they were saying, "Don't go in there. They're doing a horrible job. I was there before and it was just terrible." That's basically what online reviews are doing for businesses. That's how damaging they can be. If you see a bad review, a customer is not going to do business with them, unless they've had a positive business experience before. This is how Google has changed everything.

Another good thing about Google is the way they rank the reviews individually. If you ever wondered how Google determines which reviews pop up, we are going to tell you. If a company has several years of reviews accumulated, and you go to their website, they won't show all of them. There is just not enough room, but people can click a button to see "more" to scroll down the page. Google only shows the most recent reviews on the first page.

Even if a business had a bad start many years back, and was providing poor customer service, people can see that. If they picked up their slack and get better over time, that's awesome, but the old reviews will always be there. Negative reviews may still be affecting buyer behavior. This is why we're so adamant about reputation management!

The sooner you respond the better! If you wait too long, that customer may not even remember what they purchased or what happened. You cannot try to "fix" something that happened many years ago, but don't give up hope just yet.

Reputation Management Software

Reputation and presence go hand in hand. If you have a good presence, but there are a bunch of negative reviews then customers will likely never do business with you. Conversely, if you have a good reputation and nobody can find you because the business listing information is incorrect then you are faced with another big problem. The goal is to maximize both the visibility and the reputation for every business. Reputation management software can do this for you.

Try and do it yourself. It is very likely that you are going to get frustrated. You're also going to wonder if what you did even worked, because it is very hard to see progress over time without some type of reporting software. You can get a free snapshot of your business information and listing data from companies who offer software. Typically you cannot buy it directly, as they only allow consultants to sell it who are trained to use it. Once you're subscribed to the service, however, you will receive daily emails that let you know if somebody has reviewed your business or mentioned you anywhere online including Facebook, blogs and more. This goes back to my communication point that you want to be able to comment on any review anybody ever gives you. It's a really valuable service.

What if you have a healthy review pipeline, but you're not managing it at all? Reputation management software delivers reviews right to you, so that when somebody leaves a review, you can immediately check it out and respond. This is an immensely valuable tool available in good reputation management software. You can send customers a link to your portal, where they can leave a review which, when submitted, will disseminate too many review websites with one click.

Reputation management software allows you to view everything that's online about your business. You get an email that notifies you if you received a review or a mention anywhere online. Click the link, and it opens the page. You can see what it is, and what you need to do in terms of responding. It also finds all the places on the Internet where reviews are left about businesses such as Google+, Yelp, Yahoo, and Bing.

The software includes a mobile version of your website, that is, if your website is not already responsive. Your business information is entered the way you want to see it, and it disseminates that information out everywhere that it needs to go. When you update it once, the information distributes everywhere at the same time. Sounds pretty easy, right?

The consultant will use the software to claim every listing for you, get everything where it should be, and add your business to every spot online where you're missing on over 300 websites that list business data. Eventually, the software will get everything cleaned up and updated for you. The software reports on every aspect of things that are going on in terms of your business, so you can track progress over time.

Get your free snapshot: www.yourlastreview.com

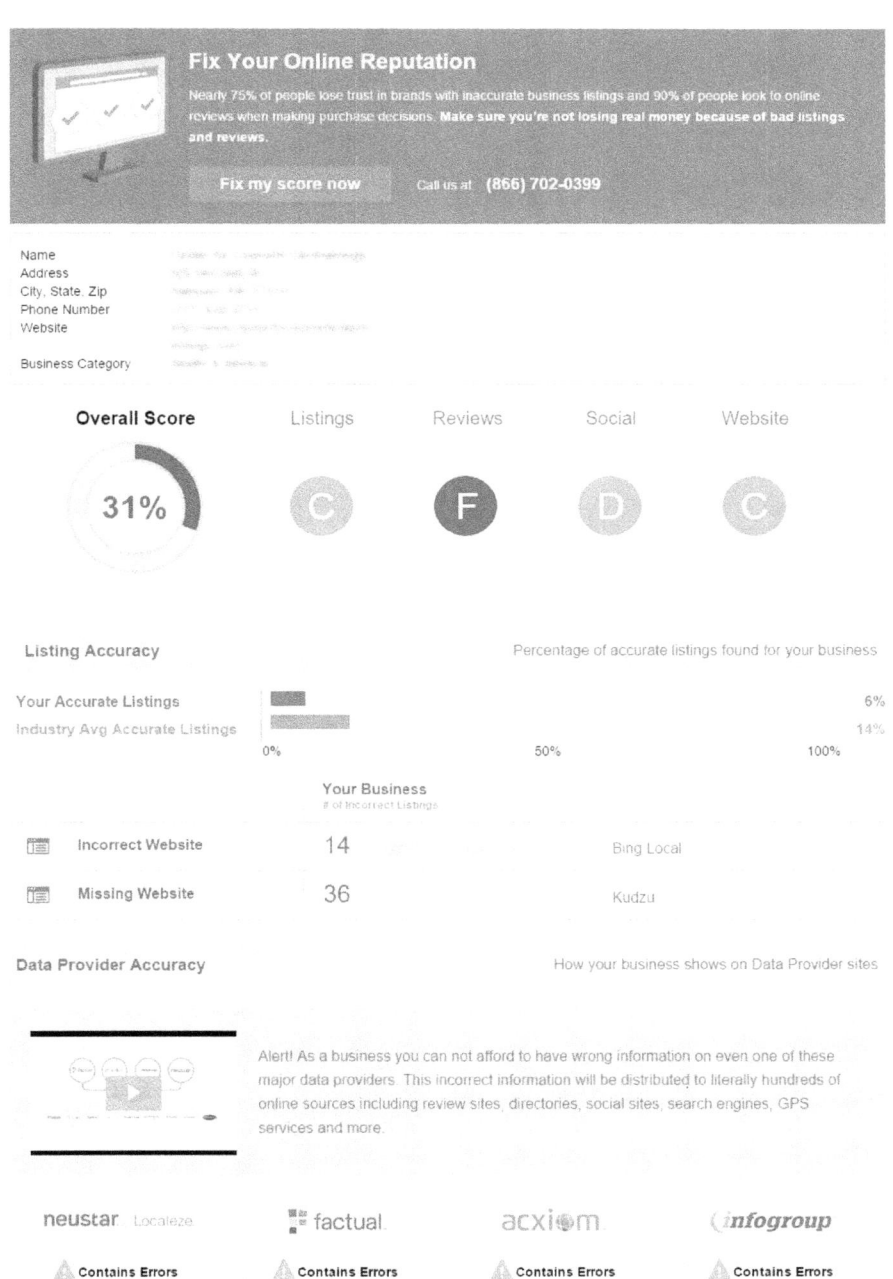

Name
Address
City, State, Zip
Phone Number
Website

Business Category

Overall Score

Listings   **Reviews**   **Social**   **Website**

31%

C   F   D   C

Listing Accuracy

Percentage of accurate listings found for your business

Your Accurate Listings	5%
Industry Avg Accurate Listings	14%

0%   50%   100%

Your Business
# of Incorrect Listings

	Incorrect Website	14	Bing Local
	Missing Website	36	Kudzu

Data Provider Accuracy

How your business shows on Data Provider sites

Alert! As a business you can not afford to have wrong information on even one of these major data providers. This incorrect information will be distributed to literally hundreds of online sources including review sites, directories, social sites, search engines, GPS services and more.

neustar Localeze   **factual**   **acxiom**   **infogroup**

⚠ Contains Errors   ⚠ Contains Errors   ⚠ Contains Errors   ⚠ Contains Errors

Get your free snapshot: www.yourlastreview.com

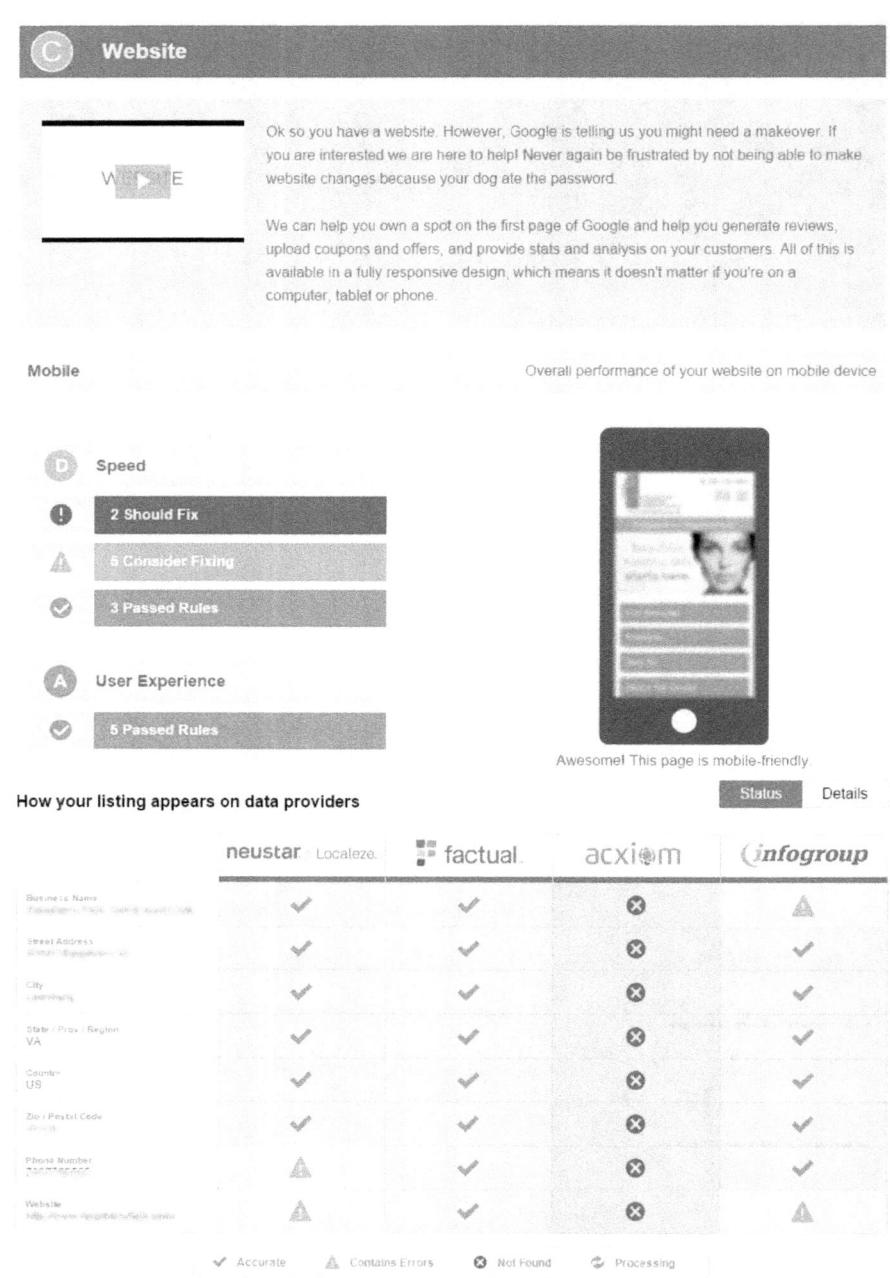

Ok so you have a website. However, Google is telling us you might need a makeover. If you are interested we are here to help! Never again be frustrated by not being able to make website changes because your dog ate the password.

We can help you own a spot on the first page of Google and help you generate reviews, upload coupons and offers, and provide stats and analysis on your customers. All of this is available in a fully responsive design, which means it doesn't matter if you're on a computer, tablet or phone.

Mobile
Overall performance of your website on mobile device

D Speed

⊘ 2 Should Fix

⚠ 5 Consider Fixing

✓ 3 Passed Rules

A User Experience

✓ 5 Passed Rules

Awesome! This page is mobile-friendly.

How your listing appears on data providers
Status   Details

	neustar Localeze.	factual.	acxiom	infogroup
Business Name	✓	✓	✗	⚠
Street Address	✓	✓	✗	✓
City	✓	✓	✗	✓
State / Prov / Region VA	✓	✓	✗	✓
Country US	✓	✓	✗	✓
Zip / Postal Code	✓	✓	✗	✓
Phone Number	⚠	✓	✗	✓
Website	⚠	✓	✗	⚠

✓ Accurate   ⚠ Contains Errors   ✗ Not Found   ⟳ Processing

Get your free snapshot: www.yourlastreview.com

Reply to All Reviews (Old and New)

If you have a negative older review on your Google+ page, and you've reformed your company's business etiquette, and so forth, you can still respond to that review. Although, you may not be able to contact that customer directly, as I said in the previous section. If there is a positive review, go through and thank the customer, no matter how old the review is. If there is a negative review, apologize and be real with your approach.

Say something like, "I know that it's 1 or 2 years later (however long it's been), but I was not aware of this comment until now, and I did not know about this page, so we are reaching out to you. I want to say how very sorry I am about your experience. Please contact me, so I can try to make it right."

Continue asking for reviews and feedback to push negative ones down. The newer reviews will still be right on top, which should be a good attempt to get as many positive reviews as possible. Continue asking for them, as well as providing a simple way for a customer to create the review.

Ask For Reviews

As part of your sales process, you should be asking for reviews and feedback. This is as simple as sending a follow up email to the customer after the transaction has been completed. If you provide a link to the page you would like them to submit their feedback, they are likely to take a few seconds to do it for you. You can create a message that you could copy and paste into an email, so it won't take you much time. Or, if you are using reputation management software, you will be provided with that message and a link directly to a page where the customer can submit it once. That review will then be submitted to many review websites.

You will start finding that your customers are some of your greatest brand ambassadors. If someone rated a product 2 stars, and made a negative comment, another past costumer may comment and suggest that they had a good experience and that they should give the company another chance. This is another reason why you want to ask for positive reviews – especially from loyal customers, patients, and clients who will stick with you until the end. They may just love to be asked for comments, and they may even get excited that you as a business owner care about their experience!

There are other, unethical ways to get rid of negative reviews, or to get more good reviews, but you must be extremely careful like I wrote before so do it the ethical way.

It might be tough to get reviews, but keep asking and making it easy for the customer to leave feedback. If someone is in a situation where they have no reviews, or a bunch of people have a lot of negative reviews, they just have to work it out with the people that left the negative ones. It is kind of a numbers game.

A method that works well is creating a postcard. Put on the postcard where you would like people to go to leave a review. Have your sales people do this as part of their sales/marketing agenda. When you hand someone an invoice ask, "did you have a good experience? We're looking for feedback. Would you mind if I send you an email with a link to a website where you can leave some feedback?"

Other ways that you could request some positive reviews is by setting up table tents, putting signs in your waiting room or bathroom, or even emailing existing customers. I did this and received a 20% response rate. I sent out an email saying, "we're looking for reviews. If you wouldn't mind providing feedback, here is a link to the place where I want you to leave a review." It only takes about 30 seconds to click that link and write something about their experience, so many people will. This may seem like extra work, but it is worth it in the long run when you start seeing positive reviews about your business. If you don't have the time, hire a reputable reputation management company to help you by using professional software.

If you are using reputation management software, you can add this to your sales process and send an email to customers after the sale with a link asking them for feedback on the service they received. This review will then get disseminated to many review websites. If you are not using reputation management software, you can still send an email to the customer with a link to your Google+ or Facebook page asking them to leave a review.

Managing Company Reviews

If you don't have a single point of contact within your large company, who will manage the reviews? Things can get lost in the system. Big mix-ups occur, especially within medical institutions.

Reviews are great management tools. A good review can allow you to give accolades to the staff. If the company is getting people to leave reviews, that's great. Try to get more reviews month after month, and use this strategy if you do have a sales staff. Have them hand out a card with a QR code that will send customers to the page to leave a review.

With reputation management software, we can monitor mentions of companies anywhere online like social media sites, review sites and even blog sites. When someone mentions the company, an email can deliver the review or the alert to multiple people in the organization. If you subscribe to the service, and someone leaves a review, the next day you will get an email that will show you the reviews and mentions that have been left.

Where And How To Populate Reviews

Create a plan and setup a system to email your customers a link to a website where they can write a review. Then, we have some advice that you should incorporate into your sales process. After you look at all the reviews on every possible site, make note of those sites that have bad reviews. If they all have bad reviews, then you might need to look at the internal procedures of your business. But, if you are confident in your business procedures, and you know that these reviews are anomalies, send your customers to the sites with the most bad reviews first, then continue going down the list.

If you have reviews on Yelp, and if there is a bad one, send them to Yelp first. Populate these types of websites with better reviews, and, obviously, try to work it out with the person that left the bad review. I would suggest starting with your Google+ page, because that one is showing up for searches as part of that magic three. If you're listing data is accurate, this is going to help you get into that area. If you have reviews, this also helps.

Chapter 5:
Business Listing Data

Listings provide information to millions of people. These business listings exist on over 300 major websites that get thousands of visitors per day. They provide information about every different type of business that exists, and some that do not exist anymore. This is a huge deal for businesses, because in most cases they don't know that their business data exists on these websites, and that it is usually, in some ways, incorrect.

Sometimes, the phone number is no longer available. Incorrect information could also be the result of old data supplied to the website before the business had a website. The website could be incorrect, and they could actually be sending people to a competitor's website. This is called a rogue listing. Businesses move, and addresses are frequently incorrect because of this.

I don't know about you, but, when I find a company I'm looking for, and I see their old address listed, it is a shame. Even if I wanted to go there, I can't. Some companies have multiple listings because the search engine didn't know which address is correct, so they listed them all. For example, a chiropractor moved a few months prior to taking a screenshot with Bing, and she realized that the old address was still there. Yahoo sometimes adds the new address and keeps the old one, unless you are actively managing the listings manually or with software.

Google Plus

Google+'s greatest use is for your business listing. It's a social media platform, so it provides a place to leave reviews, and it's another webpage for your business. The social media aspect has not become as popular as Facebook, but it is a great place to improve search engine placement, get reviews, and post information about your business.

It works much the same way as Facebook, and is important for businesses, because Google is the king of search engines. For example, if you make a page for your business, or if Google has already created your page, it is considered a business listing. Depending on how well it is optimized for your ideal search terms, you would eventually begin coming up on the search engines more efficiently, since you have optimized the listing.

Do not wait to set up, claim and update your social media sites if you already have a business, or you are a new business owner and have a name picked out. Start building your business listings and social media sites now, so your existing business data is updated and accurate. You might not instantly come up first on Google, but your chances of ranking higher are much better after this process has been completed.

You need accurate information about your business, reviews and good content on your Google+ page. Make sure your listing data is accurate everywhere. Google Business (Google+) pages are free. It's pretty amazing what Google has provided to most businesses out there, and now it is time for them to start taking advantage of this platform.

Google has provided a webpage (Google Business (Google+) page for every business that they know is on the internet. The downside is that every business on the internet is not aware of Google Business (Google+), and they're unaware that they have a page there. Or, they ignore it. Both are problems. One of my goals with this book is to help as many business owners claim, update and monitor business listings as possible. When this happens, Google will reward businesses by ranking the website higher. Ultimately, the business will receive more exposure. Once this missing puzzle piece is found, you will be found, and everything else will fall into place. At least, that is the goal.

Use the social media platform to post things about your business, and optimize those posts. Google will rank those posts for searches, so be sure they are optimized for the search terms that are most relevant to your business. This will improve your chance of having additional results for many additional searches. Do this regularly. You could even use IFTTT.com to automatically post your Facebook posts to your Google Business (Google+) profile. This tool is incredible, so definitely check it out. It automates a lot of time from consuming tasks. To get started type "Google My Business" into Google.com and go to the business page to create or claim your profile.

Being Found?

It is obviously important that you make sure your business's presence is accurate and accessible online. It can be difficult to do since there are over 300 website sources for business data to be found. If you've ever moved, changed a phone number, website address (domain name), or email address, then it's almost guaranteed that there is incorrect data many places on the world wide web. There are hundreds of websites that list businesses that you might not even know you're on.

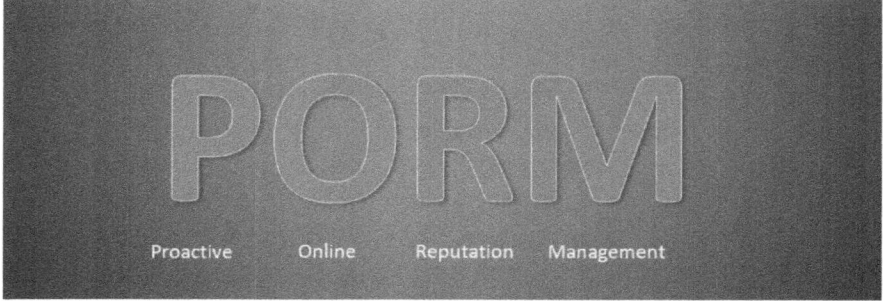

Be Proactive!

One bad review can lead to thousands in lost revenue.

PORM

Proactive   Online   Reputation   Management

Get your free snapshot: www.yourlastreview.com

I want everybody to be a PORM star, an acronym for Proactive Online Reputation Management. Sorry, I had to do it. This is a funny acronym, but it illustrates an important point. If we are not proactive about our online presence, many issues can arise that have been discussed in other places in this book. The best way to do this is to either manually monitor all 300+ websites in addition to all of the social media sites, blogs and review sites your data is found, or use reputation management software to do it efficiently.

Reputation management software helps manage your online business presence and helps business owners be proactive, so you don't have to spend hours routinely searching and submitting updated information. There are three things that every business needs in order to have a very good online presence. You need a Google+ page for your business, Google Reviews that, sometimes, you have to ask for, and consistent business listing data on your relevant online sources. Once you are on Google Business (Google+), you should be asking people to review your business. Make it easy for them by following up with an email after a transaction, or use some of the other methods discussed previously.

One of the biggest issues business people face today is being found online. One of these places is TomTom. From Google+ to TomTom, you should be listing your information. If it is incorrect, how do you change that? What about Apple Maps?

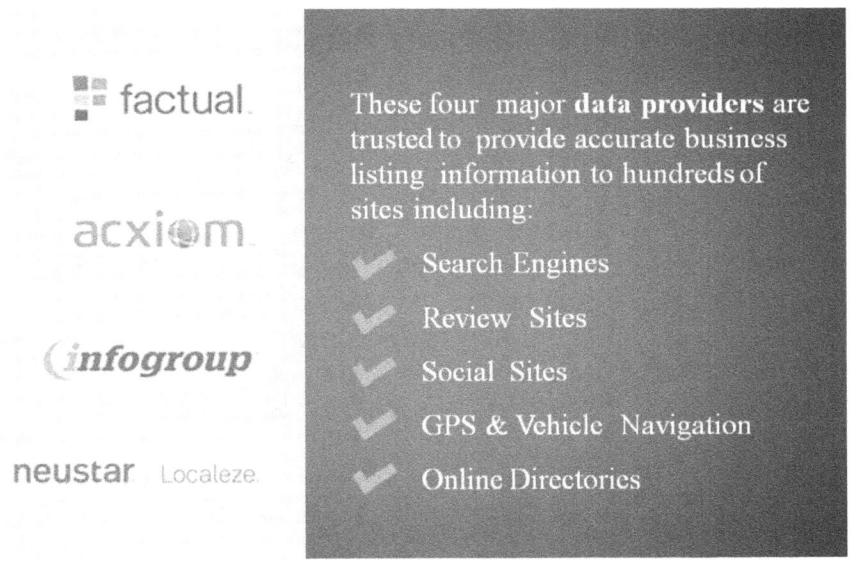

These four major **data providers** are trusted to provide accurate business listing information to hundreds of sites including:

- ✓ Search Engines
- ✓ Review Sites
- ✓ Social Sites
- ✓ GPS & Vehicle Navigation
- ✓ Online Directories

There are all kinds of different websites that are out there listing business data. Over 300 sites get their information from four major data providers, Factual, Acxiom, Infogroup and Neustar / Localeze. These data providers are trusted to provide accurate business listing information to hundreds of sites including search engine review sites, social sites, GPS and vehicle navigation. The major auto manufacturers get their GPS information from these four sources, and online directories pull their data from them.

It's not uncommon for most people to be in the dark about these four data providers. They are behind the scenes. Even the Yellow Pages are online now, but you must take action and provide them with your information. The more places you put your business information, the more likely you will be found and contacted.

You've probably heard of these major websites. Some providers that furnish information include Apple, Chrysler, Ford, Mapquest, AOL, Apple Maps, City Search, Judy's Book, White Pages, Samsung, and Toyota. You also have the Chambers of Commerce, Restaurants.com, Urban Spoon, and Sprint. This is only a small example of the 300+ websites providing business listing information.

These four major data providers send out basic business information such as your business name, street address, zip code, state phone number, website name, and business category. They are just beginning to include hours of operation, region, alternate phone numbers, and other rich business listing data. I conducted research for my own company and was surprised to see how much information was incorrect out there. How crazy is that? A guy like me who helps other businesses could have the same problem!

How your listing appears on data providers

	neustar Localeze.	factual	acxiom	infogroup
Business Name
Anthony's Books	✓	✓	✕	⚠
Street Address
1447 Ashburn Blvd.	⚠	✓	✕	⚠
City
Albany	⚠	✓	✕	⚠
State / Prov. / Region
California	✓	✓	✕	✓
Country
United States	✓	✓	✕	✓
Zip / Postal Code
90554	✓	✓	✕	✓
Phone Number
504-998-6022	✕	✕	✕	⚠

Get your free snapshot: www.yourlastreview.com

You can see that this is how you want your business to look. You want your business name spelled exactly the way it should be everywhere online. The phone number must be correct as well. Doing this manually is tedious, time consuming, and almost impossible. However, reputation management software has a direct API to these four major data providers and submits your business listing information to them, and, in turn, to all the websites pulling from them.

You can try to submit the information manually and monitor the progress. But, this will take hours per week and, in my opinion, is a huge waste of time relative to the cost of software that does it automatically. If you try to do it yourself, be sure to go back and check it frequently. Some sites will take months to update, and you never know when it fully happens unless you're logging in and checking often. Also, we have found that these data providers will sometimes revert back to the old data, so it is imperative that the data is submitted routinely. These are glitches that need to be fixed, but we are not sure if or when that will happen. Until then, we need to continually resubmit!

Rogue Listing

A rogue listing is a business listing that is partially correct. Your business is listed and everything is correct, except for the phone number, website address or the physical address. This misinformation could be sending people to your competitor. This happens more than you might think.

Bonus Case Study

A case study was created that you can view for a golf course and restaurant over a 6 month period. This study shows the positive effects of the three major areas, social, search, reputation and even how the upgrading of the website can have a positive effect on search results. Visit www.jazdesignco.com/case-study1 for the full report.

Chapter 6:
Your Website And Blogging

Next, we're going to talk about your website's assets. As I said at the beginning of this book, your website, search and social media presence all make up your online business reputation. People often cringe when I mention the word blog, because they equate that to more work, so I'll tell you how you can easily create blog content. First, let's talk about your website. If you are going to have a blog, it is better to have it attached to your website's primary domain name. Everybody should have a website if they have a business, because it is your face on the internet. It is the core of your presence online. What I mean is, everything should be directed back to your website.

Websites have evolved over the years, and, now, they need to be interactive and get people to take action once they get there. Provide something of value so people will start to know, like and trust you. Do this through free downloads, videos or even courses made available on your website. So, if you're developing a website, keep these things in mind. Instead of writing, "We're the greatest at whatever, buy from us, "it is more effective to have a Call To Action (CTA) that says, "Enter your email address, so I can send you the top ten tips on how to become a better so and so." Write a 1 page list of 10 tips. They will be the top 10 questions people ask you about what you do. This provides value to the visitor and will help generate leads from your website.

Responsive Website Design

With the advent of the mobile device, people are doing everything on their phones and they have become, in some cases, the primary device to access the internet. More than half of web traffic happens on mobile devices. This means your website needs to respond to the type of browser that's looking at it. If it's an iPhone, a tablet, or even a desktop, the website should look great and display the same information across all platforms. On each platform, it needs to look a little different, so people can use it easily. That's what responsive is. As of 2015, Google has announced that it will place preference on mobile friendly (aka. responsive) websites for searches done on a mobile device. This means that if your website is not mobile friendly, it will not show up for searches when performed on a mobile device. Google has a page that you can use to test your website to find out if it is mobile friendly. Search "mobile-friendly test" in Google to find the tool.

If someone pulls over to the side of the road to look for an address, phone number, or more information, and yours is not "mobile," they will click over to a similar business, thus interceptinga potential customer. One website is displayed differently amongst the various devices that people have. Navigating through your entire website - not just the first page, should be user-friendly. Business owners should have been aware of this years ago when smart-phones and tablets first came out. If you are still behind the times, it's time NOW to get with it.

The good thing is that you don't have to create two different websites. This used to be the case years ago. You only have to update one website in terms of articles, business data, and other pertinent information. Every website we develop is responsive, so if you need anything updated or "Jazzed up," please don't hesitate. The sooner you make changes, the better your overall reputation will be and the more business you will bring in.

Here are some tips to get your website compliant with some of Google's rules. If you're developing a website, or if you have a website, make sure your mailing address is on the first page. Also, make sure your social icons are on the first page along with your phone number. Search engines need this information to index the website for local searches.

Make your blog is part of your website. It will be mywebsite.com/blog. Please don't create a blogger.blahblah.com. It will be harder for people to find and will not help as much with SEO. Web 2.0 is the here and now. This essentially means that we're collaborating online. We are adding content to the internet now. When you add content to your blog, you are adding content to Google, and that is exactly what Google is looking for.

It used to be web 1.0. We would put a billboard up about ourselves online and people would read it. Now people are commenting on things and they're socializing. The World Wide Web continues to evolve and expand. Web 3.0 is coming. It's real exciting. Just look it up. Your voice on the internet is your blog. It's an online discussion that's started by you. What I mean by that is, you have everybody's customers, all of which have questions.

Blogging and Content Creation - The New SEO

Customers with questions are seeking the answers to these questions. What is the first thing you do when you have a question? You Google it! A blog can provide those answers. A blog is part of your website as explained above. You have the ability to add entries to the blog, and each entry is titled so that it will have an opportunity to become indexed for searches and provide answers to your ideal customer's questions.

You could create an educational platform to inform your ideal customers and your existing audience. Blogging and writing articles that link to other professional, experienced, and educational articles and websites work very well. Blogging is the best inbound marketing tool out there. If you need help coming up with topics, there are plenty of sites that have blog topic generators. Or, you could think about the top 100 questions that you've ever been asked by customers, and think about what they would type into Google in order to get that question answered.

That could be a blog title and a great place to begin. Just start brainstorming, taking notes, and fiddling with topics. You can keep re-arranging the keywords in order to come up with the perfect topic for your chosen category. You can make list-posts, include videos. As long as you can create a spot at the bottom of your blog where the visitor can navigate to more pictures, you can also create a blog that is mainly pictures with a few short words underneath each picture/image. This would make for a fantastic blog.

Numbered list posts really get attention from your target market. You can title it "7 Ways to do such and such." You can have one image or video attached, or 7 small images attached. The sky is the limit with blogging. You can also have infographics created, or make them yourself if you are an awesome graphic designer. The website Fiverr.com has good resources for infographic designers as well.

The Short of Long-Tail Keywords

Your blog title should include keywords, and, more importantly, answer questions. Brainstorm the top 50-100 questions people have asked about your product or service. Write those down in a list. Then, attempt to write answers to 2 of them per week on your blog. In no time, you will have many new articles that Google will rank for searches around the keywords in the titles. This is the easiest way to generate content. These are called long tail keywords.

You could use short tail keywords which are extremely popular. But then, you aren't one of the only companies answering questions to short tail keywords. You are among thousands, if not millions of listings, so your website will be more difficult find. Not that you shouldn't use short tail keywords. It's vital to use both in order to become established. Once you are established, however, use both long and short tail keywords in your blogs, but focus more on the long-tailed keywords. Keyword research is great for coming up with 5-10 relevant keywords that people are already typing to find what you are selling. Google has a Keyword Planner which is very handy for this.

Answering your ideal customer's questions is called SEO bait. When somebody Googles it, the search engines are going to index the answer to the questions. Google's main objective is to provide the best customer experience possible. When you go this route, you are pleasing both the website visitor/potential customer and Google at the same time.

Search Engine Optimization (SEO)

When you have a beautiful new website, the next step is SEO. One analogy for a website and SEO is buying a beautiful brand new Ferrari, but unless you put gas in it, it's not going to take you anywhere. Search engine optimization is the fuel for your website. It's not going to make it to the top of search results if you don't have the necessary fuel. The tips I explained before about blogging are a great way to build credibility in SEO results.

SEO greatly benefits a business because it drives relevant traffic to your website. If you have been blogging for personal reasons, but never used SEO, then it's likely you didn't attract many readers. The same goes for business blogs. Search engine optimization is the process of optimizing your website and internet presence in general for specific search terms, so your website comes up on search engines. But SEO is so much more than just "Keywords." Think about it. If you created messy content with no white space, no pictures or videos, and had spelling and grammar errors, most people would be repelled by your site. This regardless of how many short and long-tail keywords you used.

The content on your website needs to be fresh and current. It also needs to look fantastic. This is the other part of SEO. Even though most people may not admit it or want to believe it, these are the reasons why we always recommend that everyone create a blog. Everybody's says, "OH, I don't have time to blog." If you took out just two hours every other week to blog, that's all you'll really need.

You don't have to blog all the time. If you blog at least once or twice a month, you have fresh content on your website, and your blog will have keywords that are related to your industry. Use what you know and what is relevant to your business. Why did you go into business to begin with?

SEO is the process of mimicking a natural process. When websites are popular, people are going to link to them from many different places on the internet. These links can come from social bookmarking websites, blogs, social media website, other websites, YouTube.com and the list goes on. If we expedite that process for a website that is not as popular, we can get traction and start seeing the website move up in the search engine results pages (SERPs) for the keywords we are targeting. These are the keywords we researched using the Keyword Planner that Google provides for free.

Over time we will start to see improvement, but it all depends on how completive the search term is. If there are millions of other results for a particular term, it will be more difficult than if there are only a few thousand. You will see the number of monthly searches, and if there are more than 1000, it is

59

usually a "high" competitive term. High competitive terms are both lot to bid on and hard to rank organically.

Two clients in one day called me because customers were going to an old address. People use the internet for directions, it's a fact. Some business owners don't think people would have trouble finding them, but that's not always the case. Business data is listed on hundreds of different websites, and when you do a Google search, you will see a bunch of results appear on the Search Engine Results Pages (SERPs).

Try It: Google your business and see how many results appear on the first and second page of Google. There will likely be listings you never realized were out there and some, if not most, will have inaccurate data. This is a huge problem for businesses today, because of the various ways people search and use the results. It's a search engine optimization issue that we all face when trying to come up with the terms to target.

The best way to come up with keywords to include in our blog titles is to ask 10 of your friends what they would type in Google to find a business that does what yours does. I bet you will get 10 different variations of terms. People are generally the same in that they all use Google, but different in what they perceive to be the right phrase to search. This is precisely why it is so important to be sure everything is accurate everywhere.

The clients that contacted me said their customers found the wrong address for them. Both of my clients moved within the last year, and most of the obvious places had already been updated with the new address. Yet, they still found the old one. It takes time for Google, Yahoo, Bing, and other search engines to update each and every detail of your address.

This means they were using some source we wouldn't think most would use and ended up going to the wrong location. These were both appointment based businesses. The impact it had was significant, since it delayed all of the other customers/patients/clients that were coming in that day. This is something they could have avoided. All they had to do was proactively manage their online business listings and use reputation intelligence software.

The presence builder software is very efficient in updating the four major data sources that provide data to websites, which list and index businesses in various categories. They have to get the data from somewhere, so four sources have emerged over time. Certain websites use different providers, so it is important to make sure you have your business data updated everywhere. This is no easy task without tools. It is unbelievably difficult to do it manually. That is why software was created with API's used to directly connect with the databases and provide the data in a format that is accepted.

In order to ensure there are no instances where they revert to old data, it is submitted every week on behalf of the client. Therefore, resubmitting it routinely is vital to the overall success of your business and online listings. Compare this to the necessity of having your business listing renewed in the phone book every year. People were using the phone book exclusively before the internet, and that expense was included in every company's marketing budget.

When was the last time you picked up a phone book? The last time I saw one, my wife was throwing it in the recycle bin to get it off the counter because it is useless. We all have phones in our pocket that can access anything we want at any time, day or night. We can utilize speech to text, so Siri can just look it up for us. My business and the software I use/provide verifies that you don't have to wait for each location to accept an update.

Pay-Per-Click

Bidding on terms in Google is called Pay-Per-Click (PPC). While this book is not about paid search, I will give you a brief description of PPC. Using the same Keyword Planner tool, you can determine how much the average cost per click would be when bidding on terms. You will actually be within the Google AdWords interface when using the keyword planner tool. You can add terms to your campaign using the tool. You will set a maximum cost per click, and a maximum monthly budget for the entire campaign. When someone searches for one of these terms, your ad will appear on the right side of Google. Or, at the top of the organic column, depending on how relevant your website is for that term. It is also determined by how much your maximum cost per click and budget is in relation to other advertisers.

When someone clicks on your ad, your account will deduct the bid amount for that term. When your daily budget or monthly budget has been met, your ads will disappear until the campaign restarts or is restarted. PPC campaigns are a good way to get immediate traffic to your website, especially if it's not ranking at the top of the organic search results. Be warned, however, that just because you are getting traffic, does not mean it will convert into a new customer or a sale of a product. Test these campaigns regularly, and create many different variations to split test. When you see conversions from a campaign, you can ramp it up and start increasing the budget.

Another tip for any paid advertising is to send the traffic to a landing page. This is a page that has one call to action and usually does not have a top navigation. Decide the one thing you want someone to do when they get to the page, and make sure it is very easy for them to figure out how to do that. Create multiple landing pages to test them, and work at it until you see conversions. There are entire books written on this topic so I will stop here, but those are the basics for creating campaigns that will convert.

Chapter 7:
Marketing And Leveraging With Social Media

With social media we can reach almost any market easily, and create a large following of people who are interested in what you do. Using the blog articles you are creating, you'll create a great source for content to post on social media. You want people to find out about your company, and social media combined with blogging is a powerhouse.

There are many companies who offer both blogging and social media management services. If this is not your expertise, we recommend either hiring a professional social media manager to do it with you monthly, or hiring a one-time consultant to help you put a plan and strategy together. It's an investment, so it's not cheap, but you have to consider that both blogging and social media are crucial forms of inbound marketing and advertising. Instead of using your typical outbound marketing such as cold calling, billboards, and television advertisements, you can now split up your marketing budget on both inbound and outbound marketing. You may even want to consider spending less money on outbound and more on inbound.

In large part because of social media, the web is a social platform. Businesses need to have established social media accounts. We recommend that an account on all major platforms is established and branded. This helps with search engine optimization.

Google uses social media as part of its algorithm, since it gathers all the data from the major social sites like Facebook, Twitter, LinkedIn, Pinterest, etc. Searchengineland.com wrote, "Social signals are emerging as ranking factors as search engines determine how to leverage our social interaction and behavior." This is just one opinion on the topic, and most experts agree that having social profiles help simply because of "link juice," which is the power of having a link to your website from popular websites. When you have these active links, your brand inherently has more legitimacy. Branding and establishing your online presence is much more than creating a website or a logo.

Your links help the search engines determine which websites to rank higher than others, along with many other factors we will discuss in other areas of this book. Your social media profiles can also rank for searches, so it is very important to make sure they are optimized. Always fill out the about section completely and with good descriptions of your product or service. Got about this as if you were explaining it to someone who knows nothing about what you do. The address is very important to have accurate if you have a public location where customers can visit.

Always make sure to have the correct phone number and website address linking back to your main website from your social channels. Mobile devices use a specific category for searches, so it is important to be sure to have that as accurate as possible. This is often overlooked when setting up Facebook pages. Facebook page and profile activity also have an overall effect on your reputation and search engine optimization.

Leverage posts with keywords and descriptors for your business, as they will become indexed in Google's database. When you share new content from your blog on your social sites, you will get the benefit of having that content indexed faster. Use Facebook, Twitter, LinkedIn, Google Business (Google+) page and any other major platforms to share all of your content you post online. This attracts more attention, and is another opportunity to generate a lead if you are using call to action (CTA) buttons that go to landing pages (AKA capture forms) where people enter their information to download something of value like an eBook, for example.

When sharing this content be sure to use your business name and hashtags, so content can be indexed easily by the search engines. Hashtags are now being used on more and more social platforms like Facebook, Twitter and Instagram. They allow us to search for topics easier, index our content, and become part of a larger conversation that's already going on.

This allows our content to be found easier and for more interaction to occur around it, which is a great way to grow our presence, and, ultimately, our reputation online. One place you can go to see how you're doing as a business, or personally, is klout.com. At Klout, you can determine your score. This score is based on conversations you are involved in, the companies and people you are connected with, and your overall activity online. It uses social media analytics to rank its users according to their online social influence. To gauge how you are doing, setup a Klout profile and watch how you perform over time according to social media rankings.

Facebook, like other social media sites and apps, are visual in nature. Posting pictures of people works really well. If your customers don't mind, take a picture of them. Then, discuss what that picture means. For example, "We just did this particular job for this customer," go on to explain a short detailed account. Being personable works well, too. For instance, if you take your dog to work, you could post a picture of your "Office Buddy" just for fun. Little things like this can work well, depending on your niche.

Boosting Posts and Using Links

When you want to try to find buyers via Facebook, you want to make sure that you promote your sale posts. As an example, if you're a Realtor and have a #JustListed post that you have just put on your Facebook business page, promote that post.

There is a way to boost the post as well, or you can even do an ad for it. In some cases it is recommended that you boost posts to get in front of more people because it is extremely targeted. You can target Facebook ads and promoted posts like a laser. You can target a certain area of Branson, Missouri, if you want to. Just use the hashtags and tag relevant pages.

I am not going to get into all of the nuances of how to do all of those little things on Facebook as there are entire books written on the topic. If you tag relevant pages in your posts, it is going to get you in front of a bigger audience. You always want to develop a post with relevant data. If you have a post that you've done for a listing on your social media accounts, then share it or post it to another account on another business page. That can help out as well.

Become familiar with bit.ly or ow.ly. They are handy URL shortened websites. I recommend that everybody have an account for at least one of these if you're going to start doing any sort of social media postings. They are a really great way to make your URLs much shorter. If you have an account with them, the links are also trackable. You can go back to all of the bit.ly or ow.ly links you've created, and you can actually see how many people have clicked on your link, and where they have come from. That is actually really great information for you to have. You'll be able to see how well your posts are doing when using URL shorteners.

Getting Exposure to Your Social Media Accounts

Audience building is the backend work you'll need to tackle for social media platforms that nobody has time to do. It is extremely tedious, it takes a lot of time, and most people don't understand it. However, if you are going to start out and you are going to do it on your own, the number one thing to get started is to create a Facebook business page and share it with everyone you know. Facebook is your first line of exposure.

Your friends and family are the ones that are going to support you in your business, so you want to ask them to make sure they share your page or your account with their friends, families and colleagues. You always start there. We recommend that a business that is just starting out with a business page on Facebook, or Twitter or LinkedIn, start with some ads. They are extremely targeted. You can get yourself out there in front of your ideal audience a lot faster than promoting the organic way.

It's vital that you have your information. This includes an address, cell phone numbers, email address, and social media accounts listed on each social media account. If you don't have the addresses for your social media accounts on your printed materials like business cards, email signatures, and printed materials, you are missing a lot of targeted traffic.

Your email signature is important. You probably email lots of people in any given week. If your email signature just says, "Bob Smith," you have missed a great opportunity. Include links in your signature, so they can go straight to your website, Facebook page or LinkedIn account. Get those accounts listed on everything that you hand out to people as well. Don't miss the opportunity to let them know you have a social media presence.

Get your employees involved. Encourage the people that work with you to share, comment, or like anything that you are doing on social media for your business. They are your brand ambassadors. If you trust them enough, you can get them involved by adding them as administrators to your pages to help with posts. This is kind of a no brainer, but people think that they can't ask the people who work for them to help. They feel like they are asking too much of them. It really shouldn't be that way, because social media is here to stay. If they can go on social media for personal reasons, why not convince them to go on for business reasons?

Connect with local businesses and industry experts through social media as well. By using your social media platforms as your business, connect with those businesses that you want to work with. Also, connect with and support the businesses that may not be in your industry. One example could be the sandwich shop across the street that you have lunch at every day. Like and support that business on social media.

Like, comment and share posts as your business (not as yourself). This is something that people sometimes struggle to understand, especially on Facebook. Using Facebook as your business is a very important technique to understand. You should learn this important piece of advice, because you should be making those connections by liking, commenting and sharing as your business (not as your personal profile).

Profile Creation

Hire a respectable social media management, profile creation, and consultant who does social media management for a number of clients, which incorporates posting and doing audience building, and content creation for any social media platform. Profile creation is an a la carte service that you can also purchase. Your account will look professional and cohesive with your current website design and brand identity. Consulting is another service available, which is essentially social media training for whatever aspects of social media you wish to learn, so you can maintain your own social media accounts. The consultant should demonstrate they have helped a large number of people understand the ins-and-outs of social media that they, otherwise, wouldn't grasp.

Removing the Fear of Social Media

One goals with this book is to help take the fear out of social media. I love the quote, "Fear is nothing more than an obstacle that stands in the way of progress." I cannot tell you how many people tell me, "I don't want to do social media because I don't understand it. I don't know how to do it." I'm hoping to get rid of the idea that you "don't know how," and change your language to say, "I will learn how."

It is so important that you incorporate social media into your business marketing plan. It's here to stay, and it's where your customers are located. Like I said, I want to help you turn "I don't know how" into "I will learn how." You want to purposely create time to spend on your social media for your business.

If you aren't doing this already, start with an hour a week. Block out time on Mondays from 10:00 a.m. to 11:00 a.m. for social media. Eventually as you get used to doing it, this process is going to turn into 10-to-15 minutes per week. It really becomes second nature.

When you start out, don't just jump on every platform possible. Everybody feels like they have to be on everything. Pinterest! Instagram! Twitter! LinkedIn! You really don't. You can just start with one, figure out where your main customer base is, learn that platform really well, and when you're comfortable, add another platform to your social media presence. Knowledge is powerful – powerful enough to help remove your fear. Taking action is the next best thing. Don't just learn something and not put it into practice right away.

3 Reasons You Should Be on Social Media

There are 3 major reasons why you should be on social media. The first is immediate communication through social media. Almost everyone has a Smartphone these days. If you're a business owner and you don't have a smartphone, shame on you. The only reason I say that, is just for the simple fact that you can get notifications instantly from your business social media accounts. Not having a smartphone, or ignoring notifications in social media is a lot like ignoring a voice mail or ignoring an email. I'm pretty sure you wouldn't do that. Am I right? Nobody's going to ignore a customer's email. If you receive a notification, it means that somebody has actively engaged with your business through social media. They're expecting an immediate reply or conversation. If they're going onto your pages and say anything, you should be responding promptly.

Secondly, you need social media to brand your company. A personal brand experience is what happens when somebody goes onto your social media accounts to make a response. I had this specific experience myself. I went onto my Facebook page the other day, and I tagged a franchise that was opening a store near me. I didn't want to take an unnecessary trip and drive all the way out there, only to find they're not open yet. I posted on Facebook, "Does anybody know if this store is open?" The business responded to me, "No, we're not open yet, but we're going to be open next week and we hope that you'll come and enjoy our grand opening." I thought, "Well, that's kind of cool." They were the ones to respond, rather than me relying on my friends on Facebook. Who knows if my friends would have had the right information? Their response to me was very personable. It wasn't them throwing sale information at me or anything. They just talked to me like a person. It's really important that you act as a person and not a company when you're having Facebook conversations.

Finally, conversations are transparent. I think the biggest thing people worry about, and one of the reasons they decide they don't want to be on social media for their business, is that they're so afraid of negative reviews. To be honest, negativity doesn't occur as often as everybody thinks. But, if somebody came into your store and announced a bad experience they had, you wouldn't ignore them. You wouldn't just walk away from them. You would engage with them and do what you could to alleviate the situation.

That is exactly what you can do on social media. It's transparent, so anybody who might potentially become a customer of yours will be able to see that you can handle any type of interaction and provide excellent customer service. Likewise, if somebody says something nice to you, you want to thank them. You want to acknowledge that somebody has given you positive information and positive reviews.

Facebook

Over a billion of people in total are on Facebook. That's too large of a number to ignore. Your customers are on Facebook, so you should be as well. What are you waiting for?

Instagram

Instagram is a visual platform. It has over 300 million active users. Business have started to embrace Instagram because it has one of the most active and engaged user bases in social media. In fact, it has been reported to generate 120 times more engagement per follower than Twitter! On Instagram, it is easy and effective to share an image of a new product to ask for input.

If you sell a product, and you have a business Instagram account, you make it easier for your customers to unknowingly become Brand Ambassadors. You've surely seen someone post an Instagram picture of a meal they're eating at a local restaurant. When someone does this, they have not only the opportunity to tag the business they're at, but they can check in, too. Once someone posts a picture at a known location and tags the photo, a link instantly appears above that allows you to see any other images that have been posted to Instagram from that location. So, if you're a restaurant, Instagram is a must have social media presence, but the same goes for any business that offers a product, and, especially, if that business is one that has a storefront.

Instagram is also one of the easiest platforms for businesses to share their content across other social media platforms. Within your Instagram settings, you can enable social sharing to Facebook and Twitter, so that your photos will share automatically when you post them to Instagram.

Twitter

Twitter is primarily a B2B platform. Twitter is basically a microblog. Facebook is too, but microblogging is when people put out short bursts of information rather than long blog posts. Microblogging is when you post something on Twitter, and you put a link to your blog on your website.

Whether it's a blog or a product page, this is a really great way to get people to go to your website. It's also great for blasting out product information, industry updates, and those types of things. There are celebrities on Twitter, and it's a great news source. Twitter is usually the first place to announce any sort of newsworthy event. It's usually B2B and it's also actually something that is really good for news outlets.

LinkedIn

Everyone wants to know if they should be on LinkedIn. And you should, without a doubt. You should have a professional updated profile. You should have a fantastic headshot because if you are a business person in any way, shape, or form you should NOT have a picture of you and your cat on your LinkedIn profile. It should be something that depicts you in a professional manner.

LinkedIn is also a B2B platform. It's really great for recruiters. If you are a recruiter, or in the hiring position for your company, then you should definitely be using LinkedIn. I would tell everybody reading this to at least have a profile. If you want to start using it, then what you should do is start following industry groups. Begin participating or liking and commenting on industry group conversations. This is the basic recommendation for LinkedIn.

Google Plus

We've already talked about Google+ earlier, so I won't go into great detail here. What businesses should ideally be on Google Business (Google+)? Every single business should be on Google Business (Google+). One reason is because Google is crucial for your search engine optimization and for your Google search standings. Get a business Google listing today. You don't necessarily have to have a plan for posting and sharing at the beginning. Just create a professional account, and make sure your information is correct. Don't rush through it. This is how people make so many spelling and grammar mistakes online, which makes your business look completely unprofessional.

Pinterest

Pinterest is hugely, hugely visual. It really lends itself well to the fashion industry. Food is also another biggie. 69% of Pinterest users are female. If your ideal customer is female, you should be on Pinterest. Here's a fun fact: Garlic cheesy bread is the most re-pinned post on Pinterest. Who knew?

Using Hashtags to Promote Your Business

Where do you search hashtags? In the search box, of course. After you enter the #, enter in the term without any spaces or punctuation. If nothing comes up, it's because the hashtag is not being used. The same thing goes for Twitter, Pinterest, Facebook, Instagram, and even Google+. Hashtags are a fantastic way to find content if nothing else. Maybe you don't want to participate in the whole hashtag craziness, but it's a really great way to find relevant content.

If you want to organize pictures all in one location, use a hashtag. Photos are much easier to save with hashtags. It's a great way to organize a specific topic, whether it's a picture or another piece of content. Think about companies that hold conventions. They utilize hashtags to organize all tweets related to that convention. Hashtags are great for contests that you might want to host on Instagram too! If you're interested, we have a blog on our site about using Pinterest for hospitality businesses who want to get their customers involved in fun, creative ways to promote their companies at discounted rates.

Part 3:

Leveraging Tools

Chapter 8:
Social Media Ads

The topic of Social Media Advertisements can be a bit overwhelming at first, so I'll break it down to easier understand. Keep in mind there are entire books written on the topic alone, so we will touch on the basics. You need to create your business profile pages to create paid advertisements. If you want to do this right, you may want to consider hiring a consultant to help you set it up. There are ways to optimize and brand a page that can make a difference with overall search-ability and conversions. Let's look at some ways to test ads and focus on conversions.

If you're already on Facebook and you already have personal connections, it's a little bit easier to get started there than to start a whole new account on Pinterest, where you don't have any connections yet. That's the reason I would advise you to start with Facebook and to create a business page first. Once you understand the basics of how to use it, from there, you can move on to a Pinterest account and start pinning. When you do that, you're not just pinning your own stuff all the time, you're pinning stuff that's pertinent to your industry.

It seems overwhelming, but you're not alone. Many people, including my wife, use social media every day. I recommend that you learn how to do it, because the longer you wait, the harder it's going to be to get started. Social media isn't going anywhere. It's a major part of how people communicate and interact with businesses.

Customers want instant gratification. They don't want to pick up the phone and go through a big, long phone menu. They don't know if somebody is going to respond to an email in 2 hours or 48 hours, so it's becoming a source of contact for a lot of businesses. It's a kind of social platform.

Personal Pages Vs. Business Pages

With Facebook, you can have both a personal and a business page. The default for a Facebook business page is that you are acting as the page. When you're on your Facebook business page, you should be acting as your business. When you're on your personal Facebook profile, you should be acting as yourself.

When you're on Facebook as yourself, there's a little gear at the top right hand corner of the screen. If you click on that, a menu will appear saying, "Use Facebook as," and your page will be there. If you click on that, you'll then be using all of Facebook as your business. This means you're not going to see your friends. Your home feed is now any page that your business follows.

I always recommend that you make sure you're using all of Facebook as your business page, because you don't want to accidentally post to your own news feed. However, you can post stuff to your news feed about your business. Post on your business page, but then allude to what you've posted on your business page on your personal profile with a link. Here's an example, "Oh, you won't believe the deal that I have on my Facebook page," then provide a link. This is a call to action.

The call to action convinces people or persuades them to go to your page and take action there. You're not just blasting your friends and your family with your business, which is what you don't want to do. Your friends and your family should be your first fans. That's why you want to start a Facebook page first (if you have a profile), because you already have connections.

Facebook Ads

Next, we're going to talk about Facebook ads and the positive and negative features that came along with it. The first thing that you want to do when you're running a Facebook or Twitter ad is to determine your objective. What do you want the person to do that clicks on the ad? Where do you want them to go?

Do you want them to go to your Facebook page and like it? This is perfectly fine. Do you want them to go to a landing page where they can fill out specific information? That would be great, too. You have to determine what the objective is first.

The life expectancy of a Facebook ad is about 2 weeks. This duration is determined from what they call ad fatigue. When people keep seeing the same ad over and over again, they want to see it less and less. Switch up the image, even if you're not changing the message.

Actually, Facebook starts to display the ad less, if you don't implement change. As an example, I made three ads in the same campaign. I targeted one to people who are in bankruptcy, one to people who are going through the probate process, and one to people talking about divorce. Test your images. They allow you to upload five images. This is really a good idea to spend the time to create multiple images because you don't know what the majority are going to click on. I did a similar ad for a few days. I got 40 clicks to the website for $21. That's not too bad. The average click through rate, which you want to definitely pay attention to, was .89 and .62. If it is over a .05, that's pretty good.

Now, through Facebook's Power Editor you can also create ad campaigns on Instagram. Most users are men and women age 25 to 44 according to the statistical data at the time this book was written. If your ideal customer is of that demographic, you should consider trying some Instagram adsto target them.

Twitter Ads

You can advertise on Twitter now too. I ran an ad of my own on this social media site. This particular ad ran for five days, and we received almost two and a half thousand impressions. That's pretty good.

In order to track conversions, you have to setup tracking on your website. So, when people go there, a tracking pixel determines whether or not somebody actually took action. It is important to make sure you have enough keywords setup in your ad to get a broad enough reach. If you have only a dozen or so, you will have to increase the days in order to meet your budget in some cases.

A big tip that you can keep in mind with Twitter ads is to test the content organically first. Create a bunch of tweets with images and links. Next, see what gets shared the most, as well as what people favored the most. You'll be able to use that data to create your ad, because you can measure which one has a better conversion. To drive traffic to an opt-in page, you'll want to set up the ad differently than if you are just trying to grow your followers.

If you are trying to grow your followers, it is great to use hashtags. If you are trying just to get them to click on one thing in your ad, don't use hashtags, or any other links other than the link that you want them to click on. This is because every time they click on something, you have to pay for that. That's an important thing to learn. The page you send the traffic to should have a strong call to action, so people know exactly what to do.

Create a sense of urgency like "Buy Today" or "Get $500 for Entering." Something to create a sense of urgency and value. Include four to six tweets per campaign, so that it can optimize over time. If you are just getting started with Twitter, that will get you going.

Chapter 9
Website And Email Reputation

Reputation management comes in a few forms, reviews about your business and also the information that exists about your business on various websites. It also has a lot to do with your website and email, and how secure they are from being vulnerable to malicious attacks, which are rampant as of late.

Some websites have a database backend to support the content management system (CMS), which allows them to be easily and quickly updated in real time, as well as support many other features.

Unfortunately, there can be vulnerabilities that are found with many different aspects of the user interface that allows us to manage the website content. Every CMScan has vulnerabilities.

Even if we do our best to keep the software your website running and updated, there can be vulnerabilities detected by malicious code hackers, so there are no guarantees that the website will remain secure without some type of third party protection. This is similar to the anti-virus software you have for your local computer.

For your website, you can get a third party software that will add an extra layer of protection and reduce the vulnerabilities significantly that could exist with your website. One solution is called SiteLock. We highly recommend signing up for this protection.

There are two major reasons we are strongly recommending this. Firstly, if your website is hacked and the reputation of your IP address is compromised, your domain could be put on blacklists. It can take days or weeks to be removed from the list, and will cause your emails to go into your recipient's spam folder, or not get delivered at all.

The second major reason we feel it is very important for you to subscribe to this protection is to significantly reduce the possibility of malicious code from hackers. They can embed your website, which can potentially infect the computers of your website visitors with viruses and malware.

Think of this as anti-virus, email reputation and insurance for your website.

We have had numerous issues in the past with websites being hacked. The work involved with cleaning the website and removing the viruses and malware takes hours. In addition, you have to work to remove domain names from email blacklists, which cause on-going problems for the owner of the website.

By subscribing to the SiteLock protection, or something similar, you will have assurance that the likelihood of the website becoming compromised is significantly reduced. And if it does become compromised, it will be cleaned at no additional charge in most cases.

Resources

As stated earlier there are many websites which list business data and here are some of the ones, by category, that you will consider when ensuring your data is consistent and accurate if doing the work manually.

Search Engines: Bing Local - Google Plus Local - Yahoo! Local

Social Sites: Facebook - Foursquare - Instagram - LinkedIn - Twitter

Review Sites: Avvo - Cars.com – Citysearch – DealerRater - Edmunds - Expedia.com - Kudzu - OpenTable - TripAdvisor - Vitals - Yelp - zomato.com

Directory Sites: 411.com - Apartment Guide - Apartments.com BestLocalSearch   Better - Business Burea - DexKnows - Doctor.com – ForRent - Georgia Local Search - Health Grades - KSL Local - Local Community Guides.com - Local.com - LocalEdge - LocalSolution.com - MakeItLocal.com - Mapquest – MerchantCircle - Sunshine Media - Superpages SureWest   Texas Local Search   Yellow Book - Yellow Bot - YellowPages - Ziplocal - ypsouth.com - International Sources (Various) - 411.ca - Business.com.au - MySask 411 - N49 ProfileCanada - TrueLocal - Weblocal.ca - Yahoo! Canada Local - YellowPages.ca - YellowPages.com.au

Summing Up - What Does This Mean For Me?

What does all of this really mean for your business? The two main benefits for managing your online reputation is to respond immediately to reviews and to make sure your business listing data is accurate. The examples provided in this book show some alarming scenarios. In the Golf Course example, we were able to show people reading the review that we care. Since it was a problem, we are sure to let that dissatisfied customer know we care about what they have to say about their experience and are doing everything in our power to fix it and make it right again. This speaks volumes and can change opinions of other customers.

When a company has gone through the process to update business listing data, a number of benefits are realized. Firstly, when someone is Googling that business, they will find the accurate information and not be led to the wrong location or call a wrong phone number. Google itself will reward that business by ranking it higher in the search engine results pages (SERPs), because the data is consistent and accurate. Google wants to provide the best user experience possible, so people keep coming back. Their algorithms are structured to display information it believes to be true and accurate.

My biggest recommendation of this entire book is to start using reputation management software. There is a monthly subscription for access to it. It is worth every penny, in my opinion. It is next to impossible to do the work required to monitor and update business listing data manually. Good reputation management software has direct API interfaces with the four major data providers. This ensures that, over time, the business listing data will get updated, since it is constantly being submitted to the various websites and software programs.

See if you have any room for improvement by visiting this link: www.yourlastreview.com

Index

A

B

C

D

E

F

G

I

V

W

Y

You can request a free snapshot report for your business by visiting www.yourlastreview.com